Cooking with Jaggy

Juliana Castañeda

Illustrated by

Jenn Rodriguez

Edited by:

Luz Estella Castañeda (Spanish)

Paul Rodney Turner (English)

Designed by: Jorge Armando Ávila

Photography by: Juliana Castañeda (Jaggy)

Contributions by: Paul Rodney Turner (The food Yogi)

This Book is dedicated to my grandfather Julio, who taught me all about love.

To Srila Prabhupada, who taught me that food has a superior taste, when it is prepared and offered in devotion.

To all the non-humans animals, who gave me their unconditional love, and who allowed me to express my love for them.

Juliana Castañeda (Jaggy).

To God, who is my guide,
my family, my support
My doggies and Jorge, my love..

Jenn Rodriguez A.

Acknowledgements

I'm always grateful with many animals, human and non-human.

Two years ago, a person with whom I am most grateful, left this world. He was a person who loved good food and who understood exactly how food can unite us; a person who connected everything with food, so much so that everywhere he went he brought food with him; a person who never hesitated to offer me the food I wanted.

He was my grandfather Julio, a smart, handsome, funny, fantastic, incredible man. Whenever I saw Grandpa his first words were always, "What do you want eat?" He was such a perfect gentleman.

I've always had a special connection with food and this is largely due to my mother, an expert woman in the culinary arts who conquered hearts with her recipes and her creative inventions in the kitchen. She was always patient with me, allowing me to use her kitchen even as a child of 5 years! She gladly organizing my mess, bought the ingredients, and was always ready to strongly critique everything I cooked so that I could improve. Thank you mother.

A warm thanks goes to my long time friend Ekala Isvara das, a lover of desserts, expert baker, and a great person to work with in the kitchen. He is one of the people who gives me strength to continue creating in the kitchen. For him, all my efforts in the kitchen are perfect.

My aunt Sita introduced me to one of my favourite cuisines, Hare Krishna gourmet, allowing me to elevate my passion for food to the pure dimension of cooking with bhakti (devotion to God), wherein all my efforts were centred on pleasing God as the Source of everything I prepared; the Source of all enjoyment, and my number one guest.

My grandmother Ligia does not like to cook, but her undying love for my grandfather Julio motivated her to cook a special feast every Sunday for him. We could all taste her love and it touched our hearts deeply. Thank you for your this wonderful experience.

Although I took a different path than what he aspired for me, my father Germán always allowed me to follow my heart. For that I am very grateful.

My spiritual master, Guru Prasad Swami – my shelter, my guide, my judge, my spiritual father, thank you.

To Paul Rodney Turner (Priyavrata das), the "food yogi" for loving me, protecting me, taking care of me, educating me and helping me to make my dreams come true. You are my super hero.

I've always knew that food has the power to unite, but some unions are not eternal. There is one union, thanks to food, that evolved like a great 'recipe' over time, and that is my connection with my friend Camilo. He has always been patient with me. My relationship with him is one of my favourite 'recipes' in life – a friend whom I don't give much attention to these days because I am so immersed in my projects.

Finally, to all the non-human animals in the world, whom I respect, love, admire, imitate, dream about, and live for, because I never want them on my plate – I only want them in my heart. A huge thanks to them, because without the unconditional love I constantly receive from them, I would never have understood the meaning of real love. This book is a way to reciprocate all the love they have given to my life.

Juliana Castañeda (Jaggy).

Foreword

One of the things that struck me most about Juliana ("Jaggy") is her absolute dedication in the kitchen and her passion to please others. "I am a servant," she often tells me. Frankly, you don't often hear that sort of comment from talented people. But Jaggy devotedly adheres to this philosophy on life and delights in seeing the happiness of others.

This same attitude can be seen in her work with animals at her Paramatma Animal Sanctuary in the Andes Mountains. "They are my babies," she says of the 34 animals she rescued from abuse. It is refreshing and delightful to come across a soul like hers; one that can light up a room when given a chance, but if not, is perfectly happy to gently burn in the corner away from the attention of the world.

What you'll find in this book is a selection of her best recipes, crafted over 27 years of artistry in the kitchen. Yes, Jaggy is only 32 and has been cooking since she was only 5 years old! The recipes are fun and innovative but packed with nutritional punch, so you can be sure you're getting real nourishment for your body, mind and soul.

Each recipe is illustrated by the talented Jennyfer Rodriguez who has tried to capture the mood of the recipe with her unique style. Every recipe was tested by me, and as a chef myself, I offered suggestions where necessary, but honestly, I was more than once, fully blown away by what Jaggy created from the simplest ingredients.

What makes this cookbook unique, however, is not just the wide selection of recipes, coupled with captivating photography and accentuated by groovy illustrations, is the soulfulness of each recipe. You see, Jaggy was trained in a very ancient culinary tradition, the same one I was, the Vaisnava culture of hospitality.

This tradition prides itself on using cooking as a way to communicate with the Divine, and this devotional art form is expressed in temples all over the world. Jaggy learned this art form at a very young age and has embraced the essence of that art form ever since, even while playing with different food cultures.

The Vaisnava culture of hospitality is based on the belief that all beings are spiritually equal and that the most fundamental way to express that truth is through the sharing of pure food. What constitutes "food pure," however, can be a topic of philosophical debate, but essentially, it means food that is both physically and energetically pure. How do we achieve that? By preparing the meal with loving intention for the purpose of pleasing the Divine and then making an offering of that food to God before eating it ourselves. Such intuitive and selfless cooking requires discipline and that is exactly what Jaggy learned from age 5.

I promise you this: What you will take away from this cookbook is much more than you may first imagine. You will be pleasantly thrilled with the results and my hope is that you can share these new culinary gems with your family and friends and thus inspire Jaggy's flame of love to enlighten as many people as possible.

Paul, the "Food Yogi"

www.foodyogi.org

Food for Life Global Director

www.ffl.org

Introduction

While giving one of my vegan gourmet cooking classes, one of my students approached me and asked if we could do a cookbook together that included her artwork. My student Jennyfer Rodriguez is a Colombian artist who has a unique illustration style, so in that moment was born the idea of Colombia's first vegan cookbook.

For a long time I have wanted to do a cookbook, but collaborating with Jennyfer seemed to present the perfect opportunity to do something special – something that could capture all the senses and set this cookbook apart from the others. For me, the best part of cooking is being able to enthral all the senses.

I don't want to just give a different way of healthy eating; I aspire that everyone embrace a new way of eating that nourishes their body, mind and soul.

Food is fundamental to our life; it unites and has the power to build relationships, but to do this really effectively, the food must be pure and as natural as possible. Therefore, the golden rule in my kind of cooking is: do everything with love. Our food should never come from the suffering and pain of others and that is why a long time ago I chose to eat a plant-based diet.

When we use ingredients that involve the killing of non-human animals, knowingly or unknowingly, we include their pain and suffering as well, and thus give these same negative emotions to our family and friends. In this way, we can't possibly deliver the pure message of love. We may be cooking to flatter our guests; to please our partner or nurture our children, and all of these acts may be done out of love, but the purest love is a love that respects and honours all, even those who do not have a human body – the animals. .

Like us, they also know how to feel and give love. To ignore this fact is to miss the real truth of cooking with love.

This book is one of my gifts of love to the world. It is an invitation to expand your love by starting to love yourself and then expanding this wonderful energy to all our food preparations, so that you can take everybody you feed to a place of peace, respect and fulfilment.

My hope is that the small steps you'll take in your kitchen will help the people around you return to their core truth – that we are all equal, regardless of the external form we are occupying, and that what makes us most happy is when we learn to serve others with love.

I have two secret ingredients in my cooking: I never taste my preparation until it is completely finished; and when it is completed, I offer this loving creation with a prayer or a sacred mantra to the Source of all love and all food: God. My meals then become 100% sanctified, or prasadam, which is a Sanskrit word that means mercy. It is something I learned in my early days of cooking in bhakti yoga temples. When we make our meals with the intention of pleasing God, the food becomes purified of all negative energies and nourishing to our body, mind and soul.

So let's have some fun in the kitchen! Try these recipes and share them with all those you love and even those who are not your "best friends." Why not? I assure you that everything will change once you offer others the best food with the best intention. Even so-called "enemies" will become your friends.

Thank you for starting this journey with me. I promise you this: once you see the power of cooking with love, you will never return and will want to be on this journey forever.

- Juliana Castaneda (Jaggy)

Paramatma Animal Sanctuary.

Like many children in the world, I was always an animal lover, and like many children I had a dream: "When I grow up, I want to have a big place to help animals." I'm sure if some of my childhood friends or family read this, they will remember perfectly.

I have a clear idea of why I come to this world: I was born to be a servant…that means helping others be happy and safe. I believe that success of my life can be measured by the positive contributions that I have made to others.

My greatest desire is to help the innocent, and I think the animals are the most innocent. Because they have a different language and can't ask for help or protect themselves, they are like children and so are more innocent than humans.

With this desire in my heart, after many adventures, overcoming many challenges, and learning so many wonderful lessons I finally did it! With the help of two very dear friends and the strength and loyalty of one in particular, Ekala Isvara das, we purchased a property and this dream came true.

The animal sanctuary I co-founded and co-direct, has 34 animals, not just dogs and cats, but also a fighting cock, a horse, a lab rat, a lab rabbit, a quail, and the only cow and bull protected in my country. We have the only animal sanctuary in the country that protects domestic and non-domestic species, and the second in South America that has protected cows.

We called this animal sanctuary Paramatma, which is a Sanskrit word that means, "God in the heart," and in this way, Ekala and I try to teach the world of the spiritual equality of all beings.

Each of the animals was rescued from an unpleasant situation, but now each one enjoys the freedom, love and protection that any child deserves.

This is my dream come true. This is my love project, and an example of how a little woman like me with determination, strength and love, can achieve her dream and give protection to those in need.

Paramatma Animal Sanctuary is not an easy project. We are currently the only two volunteers. We want to continue this dream and thank you dearly for helping us. You see, **by purchasing this book, 60% of the profit goes directly to Paramatma Animal Sanctuary.**

But there are even more ways to help: please visit our website and social media page and help us spread the voice of those who do not speak our language.

Thank you very much.

Menu

Main meals	1
Soups	2
Raw	3
Salads	4
Bakery	5
Desserts	6
Smoothie	7
Recipes For Animals	8

Main Meals

Spinach and Marinated Mushrooms

Since I was a little girl one of my favorite vegetables was spinach. I remember when I was 8 years old one of my aunts made a special salad that just had spinach, sesame and lemon, but for me it was like being in heaven. So for you spinach lovers here is a super simple recipe that you can serve with rice, toast or bread.

Recipe for 4 people.

Ingredients:

1 Tbsp. olive oil

2 Tbsp. coconut oil

10 fresh bay leaves

2 Tbsp. chopped fresh thyme

500 grams of fresh mushrooms (you can choose your favourite mushroom). Wash and cut into medium slices.

300 grams of fresh spinach, chopped

½ yellow bell pepper

1 tsp. grated ginger

½ tsp. Tumeric powde

3 Tbsp. vegan cream

Sea salt

Preparation:

Sauté the bell pepper in coconut oil with thyme and bay leaves for about 2 minutes on a medium flame.

Next, add the mushrooms and ginger and continue to sauté for another 10 minutes. (Be careful not to burn anything).

Next, add chopped spinach, vegan cream and tumeric. When the spinach is soft, turn off the flame. Add salt to taste and enjoy!

Tip: Did you know that spinach helps fight tooth decay and prevents oral infection!

Quinoa Pilaf with Broccoli

Quinoa, the food that is on everyone's mind... either to eat or to talk about their fantastic new recipe, or the multitude of ways we can use it. Entering the world of quinoa, I offer this recipe, which was born from my love for quinoa and my unbridled passion for pistachio.

Recipe for 4 people.

Ingredients:

1 cup quinoa

4 cups water

2 cups broccoli cut small pieces

2 Tbsp. lemon juice

1 tsp. balsamic vinegar

1 Tbsp. lemon zest

2 Tbsp. olive oil

½ Tbsp. grated fresh ginger

½ tsp. dried thyme and bay leaf

1/3 cup raisins

¼ cup finely chopped parsley

½ cup lightly toasted pistachios

Pink salt to taste

Preparation:

Boil 4 cups of water in a big pot with the thyme and bay leaf. Add the quinoa and reduce heat to medium flame and cook with the pot covered for 10 minutes.

Remove pot from the heat and let stand for 10 minutes.

Remove excess water and transfer quinoa to a large bowl.

In a separate pot steam the broccoli until the broccoli is still slightly firm and then add to quinoa.

In another bowl, mix lemon juice, olive oil, ginger, pistachio, salt and lemon zest.

Pour this dressing into the large bowl with quinoa and broccoli, and garnish with raisins and parsley.

Tip: Quinoa is one of the most complete plant foods containing nine essential amino acids (proteins).

*Caramelized Beans and Corn stir fry
with Coconut, Mint and Lemon*

Just thinking of something with caramelized corn, coconut and mint sounds fascinating, right? And this dish is easier than you think. It is bursting with all kinds of flavours and looks super dramatic when completed.

Recipe for 4 people.

Ingredients:

1 pound of green beans cut into 1 inch
pieces

4 cups fresh corn

1 ½ Tbsp. coconut oil

1 Tbsp. coconut sugar or brown sugar

¼ Tbsp. salt

1 Tbsp. fresh lemon juice

1/3 cup of dried coconut flakes

1 tbsp. mint or spearmint leaf

Preparation:

In a wok or skillet on a low to medium heat, add coconut oil and sauté beans, corn, brown sugar and salt for about 30 minutes until beans and corn appear caramelized, but not burnt.

In a separate pan gently roast coconut flakes in coconut oil over a low flame until lightly browned.

When the beans and corn are caramelized, add a serving portion to a bowl, add a squeeze of lemon juice and then garnish with toasted flakes and chopped mint or peppermint leaf. Serve warm.

Tip: Beans help to regulate glucose, so they are perfect if you are on a low-fat diet and very useful if you have problems with fluid retention.

Marinated Potatoes
with Roasted Peanuts

I confess! I'm a fan of potatoes – all types and sizes. It must be my Colombian roots because potatoes are a staple of many recipes. I could eat potatoes all day, fortunately, carbs are not my enemy and I am able to keep a slim waist.

I enjoy this very simple recipe at least once a month. I'm sure you will love it too.

Recipe for 4 people.

Ingredients:

1 pound of medium-sized white
potatoes

1 pound roasted peanuts

1 pound tomatoes

1 tsp. dried thyme and bay leaf

5 mint leaves

Preparation:

Wash, peel and cut potatoes into 4 pieces each. Boil in water until soft.

In another pot, add tomatoes to boiling water until the skin cracks. Then run

under cold water to remove skin. Next, add the blanched tomatoes to a blender and liquefy.

Pour tomato blend into a pot and add chopped roasted peanuts, thyme and bay leaf.

Once the potatoes are cooked, mix with the tomato blend, add mint leaves and cook for

additional 5 minutes on a low flame.

Tip: Potatoes are high in fiber, which supports healthy digestion and protects the body from

colon cancer. They also contain Vitamin B6, which helps with cell renewal, a healthy nervous

system and a balanced mood.

Eggplant and Plantain Sizzler

Many people are afraid to eat eggplants, while others have never tried them or have had a terrible experience. But I assure you, this recipe is fantastic and you will fall in love with eggplants like never before.

Recipe for 4 people.

Ingredients:

3 eggplant chopped in cubes

1 plantain

4 tomatoes

1 tsp. dried thyme and bay leaf

1 tsp. turmeric powder

½ red bell peppers

Coconut oil

Preparation:

First soak the eggplant in salted water. Fill a pot of water sufficient to cover our eggplants cubes and add a teaspoon of sea salt. Allow them to soak for 30 minutes. Discard the water. This soaking process helps to remove the acidity of the eggplants.

Next, cut the plantains into cubes, the same size as the eggplant and add them to the same pot. Add water to cover and cook on a medium flame until they are soft. Discard the water again.

In a blender, liquefy tomatoes with thyme, bay leaf and turmeric.

Next, cut the bell pepper to size you prefer. Fry them in a pan with coconut oil, a little thyme and dried bay leaf.

Add the liquefied tomatoes to the bell peppers and cook on a low to medium flame for 10 minutes

Add the tomato and bell pepper gravy to the cooked eggplants and plantains and mix well. Heat for an additional 2 minutes on a medium flame.

Tip: Eggplants are a great antioxidant. They promote blood circulation; lower cholesterol, prevent arteriosclerosis; help eliminate fat, and inhibit the growth of cancer cells in the stomach due to the presence of vitamin E.

Soups

Carrot Soup with Coconut Cream

I love carrot juice, carrot cake, and raw carrots! They are wonderful because they are both sweet and salty at the same time. The flavour is divine. Here is a simple soup bursting with flavour and nutrition.

Recipe for 4 people.

Ingredients:

5 carrots chopped in ¼ inch cubes

1 ½ cups of coconut cream

2 Tbsp. coconut oil

½ yellow bell pepper finely chopped

½ tsp. dried thyme and bay leaf

½ tsp. minced ginger

1 cup almond milk or your favourite non-dairy milk

Salt to taste

Preparation:

In a pot place the coconut oil and stir fry thyme, bay leaf, ginger, and finely chopped yellow bell pepper on a low heat until lightly braised (do not overcook).

Next add diced carrots and stir fry for 1 more minute.

Next add coconut cream and continue cooking on low heat for another 10 minutes or more until carrots are soft.

Once carrots are soft, add everything to a blender, add non-dairy milk and liquefy the mixture.

Return the hot liquid to the pot, add salt cook for another 10 minutes on a low heat.

Tip: Coconut milk is rich in Zinc, which plays an important role in the functioning of the prostate and helps reduce the risk of cancer cell formation.

Apple and Avocado Soup

Is there anything better than avocados and apples? Yes! A creamy soup made from apple and avocado. This is a great combination of two beautiful fruits. Few people use avocados in hot preparations. Avocados are almost always used as an accompaniment, and apples are typically something you eat alone. With this recipe, however, you'll discover that an avocado is more versatile than you imagined.

Recipe for 4 people

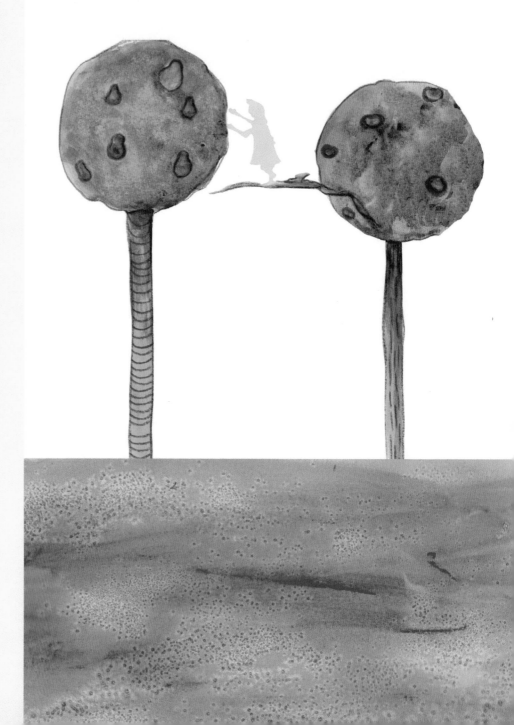

Ingredients:

2 avocados cut into one inch cubes

3 green apples, peeled and cut into one inch cubes

½ Tbsp. minced ginger

½ Tbsp. dried thyme and bay leaf

½ Tbsp. coconut oil (you can also use pure sunflower oil)

2 cups water

4 tsp. pure olive oil

1/4 cup parsley

Salt to taste

Brazil nuts chopped fine

Preparation:

In a pot large enough for 4 cups of soup, on a low flame add coconut oil and fry the thyme, bay leaf and ginger.

In a blender, blend apples, avocado and parsley with water until you have a creamy mixture. Add this mixture to the pot, add salt and stir.

Cook for 15 minutes over medium flame mixing constantly.

Serve garnished with parsley and chopped nuts.

Tip: Scientific research published in the journal Nature, suggest that apples have anti-cancer and antioxidant properties. Their anti-cancer properties, especially for the skin, is due to the presence of phytochemicals.

Tofu, Broccoli, Tomato Soup

Yes! Another treat with tomatoes, excellent! My sister does not like broccoli and to avoid the broccoli she tells everyone that she is allergic. But with this soup, she decided not to be allergic.

Recipe for 4 people.

Ingredients:

1 small broccoli, chopped

3 large tomato cut into thick slices (½ inch)

1 Tbsp. coconut oil or other vegetable oil

½ Tbsp. minced ginger

½ pound soft tofu

½ tsp. turmeric powder

½ tsp. paprika powder

½ Tbsp. finely chopped cilantro

1 cup water

Salt to taste

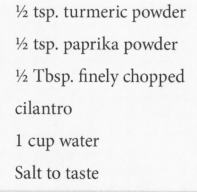

Preparation:

First let's BBQ some tomatoes. Place the slices in a pan with just a little oil and cook on a low flame for 10 minutes, turn them over as needed. Do not burn them. What you want is a "BBQ" tomato.

While the tomatoes are cooking, continue with the other part of the preparation.

In another pan, put a little oil, ginger, paprika, turmeric, salt, tofu and broccoli over medium-low flame and stir-fry for a few minutes. Then lower the heat and cook slowly for 1 minutes (If needed, you can add a little water)

Once the tomatoes are browned on both sides, take them to the blender. Next, add the BBQ tomato sauce to a large pot, then add the pan-fried vegetables and let simmer for another 15 minutes.

Tip: The two main components of tomatoes, p-coumaric acid and chlorogenic acid, which are essential in fighting against nitrosamines produced in the body by smoking and are the main carcinogens in cigarette smoke.

Avocado and Mushroom Soup

Yes , here we go again! For the lover of avocado and mushrooms. I have a fantastic marrying of two robust vegetables in a delicate soup with an elegant texture.

Recipe for 4 people.

Ingredients:

3 ripe avocados

350 grams of mushrooms sliced

1/3 cup of olive oil

1 Tbsp. coconut oil (you can use other vegetable oil,

but nutritionally and for a better taste, I recommend coconut oil)

Salt and pepper to taste

1 large tomato finely chopped

½ tsp. of cloves

1 cup of water

1 tsp. minced ginger

Preparation:

In a large pan, add coconut oil and sauté 250 grams of mushrooms, cloves and ginger for 10 minutes. Next lower the heat and add finely chopped tomatoes, stirring regularly for 10 minutes.

In a blender or preferably a food processor blend the remaining mushrooms, avocados, olive oil adding water in parts to help with the blending until you get a creamy texture. Be sure that the mixture is not too thick like a pudding, so add more water if needed. What you want is a creamy liquid.

Add this creamy liquid to the large pot and cook on a low heat for 10 minutes.

Serve garnished with finely chopped fresh mushrooms and parsley.

Tip: Did you know that avocado is good for your eyes! This is due to a carotenoid called lutein. Avocado absorbs ultraviolet rays from the sun thus preventing them from harming the retina. It also protects the eyes from degeneration and cataracts.

Lemon Spinach Potato Soup

Soup with a hint of lemon to fire up the senses on a boring day. It's the kind of soup you can eat in the winter or summer months. This soup is simple to make, but delicate and elegant to share with family and friends on special occassions.

Recipe for 4 people.

Ingredients:

4 cups spinach, chopped

4 cups almond milk (you can use any non-dairy milk, but for a

delicate flavour I recommend almond milk)

4 potatoes, peeled and cut into small cubes

1 cup shelled corn

½ tsp. coconut oil

¼ lemon juice

½ tsp. minced ginger

4 cinnamon sticks

Salt and pepper to taste

Zest of one lemon, chopped finely

Preparation:

Boil the potatoes until soft.

In another pan, add coconut oil and on a medium flame, sauté the spinach, corn, cinnamon sticks, salt and pepper for 3 minutes. Lower the heat and continue cooking for another 10 minutes with a lid on top.

Next add the boiled potatoes to this same pan and cook for another 5 minutes.

Then transfer the contents of the pan to a blender, add almond milk and process until thoroughly mixed.

Transfer this liquid to a pot and on a low flame warm it for 10 minutes. Then mix in the lemon juice juice.

Serve garnished with lemon zest.

Tip: Lemon ranks first among curative fruits. It is a great eliminator of toxins and a powerful anti-bacterial. According to one study, fresh lemon juice and peel inhibits the growth of V. cholerae.

3

Salads

Spinach Mango Salad

By Paul Turner, The food yogi

One day I was in a raw food masterclass at the Living Light Institute in California and one of the salad recipes caught my eye, a summer kale salad. It was so unique and tasty.

I decided to make a colombian version of his salad using spinach. This salad has all the flavours: salty, sweet, sour, pungent and astringent. It overwhelms the taste buds and just electrifies any meal you serve it with.

Yield: 4-6 people

Ingredients:

1 x bunch of spinach cut into fine strips

1 x nori sheet cut into fine strips

1 x fresh red romaine lettuce

1 x red bell pepper finely chopped

1 x large avocado cubed

1 x carrot grated

1 x mango cubed

Dressing:

¼ cup virgin cold pressed olive oil

1 Tbsp. apple cider vinegar or lemon juice

¼ cup tahini

2 tsp. coriander powder

1 tsp. paprika powder

1 tsp. cayenne pepper

¼ cup agave syrup or maple syrup

1 tsp. sea salt

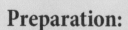

Preparation:

1. Mix all ingredients in a bowl

2. Marinate finely chopped kale for 5 minutes, using your hand to massage the spinach, before adding all the other ingredients, including the nori sheets cut into fine strips.

Paul, the food yogi, has gifted this récipe as well. He writes: "This salad is a more classic Italian salad perfect for a hot summers day. It is light and refreshing with just the right ingredients to compliment a summer lunch of pasta and bread.

This salad was inspired by my early cooking teachers during my time as a monk in the temple. We would serve a similar salad for our lunch time guests at the temple."

Yield: 6 servings

Ingredients:

1 x green lettuce chopped

1 x red lettuce chopped

1 x yellow bell pepper finely chopped

4 x large tomatoes

1 x cup chopped palmetto

½ cup green olives

Dressing:

¼ cup virgin cold pressed olive oil

¼ cup flax oil

¼ cup purified water

3 Tbsp. lemon juice

2 tsp. agave syrup or maple syrup

1 tsp. Italian seasoning

½ tsp. sea salt

Preparation:

1. Mix all ingredients in a bowl, except tomatoes and olives

2. Gently stir dressing through mix

3. Garnish with tomatoes and olives

Mom's Hearty Pasta Salad

There is nothing better than mom's cooking and it's because a mother cooks everything with unconditional love and a sincere desire to please the family. The basic ingredient, which should not be a secret, is love.

My mother Clara always makes this cold salad and it's very delicious.

Yield: 5 people

Ingredients:

550 g pasta (vegan) spiral

3 large white potatoes, peeled

1 large carrot

1 pound fresh green peas

2 fresh tomatoes

¼ pound of soft tofu

1 cup vegan "ham" cut into cubes

Dressing:

1 cup unsweetened soy milk

1 cups sunflower oil

¼ cup lemon juice

1 pinch of salt

Preparation:

Cook pasta, strain, wash under cold water and set aside.

Peel carrots and potatoes and chop each into small ½ inch cubes.

Cook carrots, potatoes and pees until soft, strain and set aside.

Cut tomatoes into small pieces. Then mix all ingredients, including tofu in a large bowl.

To make the dressing:

Mix the milk with half cup of sunflower oil. When well mixed, add another half cup of oil and mix again until you get a thick consistency. Next, add the lemon juice and mix well.

Add dressing to the bowl of salad and enjoy!

4

Baking

Coconut, Carrot, Nut Muffins

There are many vegan muffin recipes, but this is my personal recipe and I confidently declare: "It is divine." The mixture of flavours and the soft and crunchy texture creates a fun experience for the palate.

It is simple to make, cheap, and ideal for all occasions.

Makes enough for 10

Ingredients:

500 grams wheat flour

250 grams maize meal

300 grams peeled carrots

100 grams roasted sunflower seeds (15 min in the oven at 170 °)

10 Tbsp. coconut oil

10 Tbsp. warm water

20 grams baking powder

The peel of half a lemon, chopped fine

5 grams salt

100 grams brazil nuts, chopped

60 grams desiccated coconut

1 tsp. ground cinnamon

1 cup Soymilk

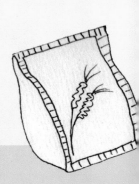

Preparation:

In the food processor, add carrots, salt, cinnamon, and orange peel. While processing, slowly add sunflower seeds, coconut and melted coconut oil.

Then in a bowl, add wheat flour, maize meal, and baking powder and mix well. Next, add the contents of the food processor to this bowl and mix by hand until the dough is tender and falling gently. If necessary you can add more soymilk to achieve the right consistency. Next, add the chopped nuts and mix everything well. Pour the batter into muffin tins and bake at 180 ° for 25 minutes.

Pistachio Cookies

I have never met a person who does not like pistachio. I think it is a favourite nut of many people. And I have never met a person who says: "I don't like cookies."

This special combination of two very dear "friends" is sure to please everyone.

Serve with tea, coffee or just a smoothie.

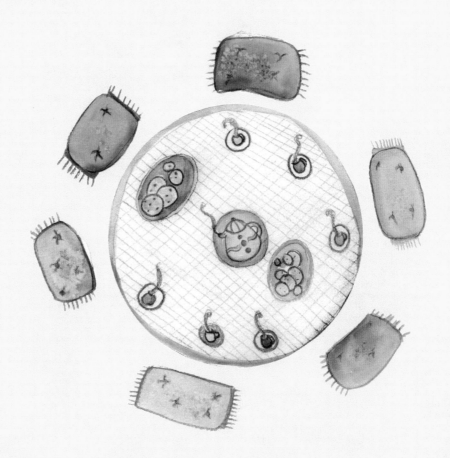

Ingredients:

200 grams of flour

100 grams of chopped pistachios

3 Tbsp. sugar

½ tsp. cardamom

5 Tbsp. olive oil

2 Tbsp. coconut water

Preparation:

Preheat oven to 300 C

In a bowl, mix oil, flour, sugar, coconut water and cardamom powder.

Knead well.

Next, add chopped pistachios and form balls the size of plums.

Grease a baking tray with oil and bake the cookies for 20 minutes.

*Peanut Butter Chocolate Chip
Banana Bread*

I think banana, peanut butter and chocolate is the perfect combination. For me it's like being in heaven! It's something celestial, healthy, and very delicious. Bananas are one of my favourite fruits. They have the perfect combination of sweetness and texture, and they go well with just about everything.

Recipe for 1 loaf of bread

Ingredients:

5 bananas

2 Tbsp. olive oil

2 cups whole wheat flour, sifted

1 tsp. salt

1 tsp. baking powder

½ cup brown sugar or coconut sugar

¾ creamy peanut butter

1 tsp. vanilla extract

1 cup of your favourite non-dairy milk

1 cup vegan dark chocolate chips

Preparation:

Preheat the oven to 350 C

In a bowl, mix the bananas and olive oil to a consistency like mashed potatoes.

Next, add the sugar, vanilla, salt and baking powder and mix everything well.

Then add the whole wheat flour, vegetable milk and mix.

Finally, add the peanut butter and dark chocolate chips.

Coconut, Oat Scones

These scones are perfect for all occasions and can be served with hot or cold drinks or just as a snack to take on the go. They are simple to make, delicious and hearty snack when you feel hungry.

The coconut gives it a cool, tropical feel, while the oats provide the crispy texture.

You'll love it!

Recipe for 15 servings

Ingredients:

2 cups almond flour

1 ½ cups of oatmeal powder

1 cup ground flaxseeds

½ cup desiccated coconut

2 Tbsp. brown sugar or coconut

sugar

2 Tbsp. baking powder

1 teaspoon sea salt or pink salt

1/3 cup melted coconut oil

¼ cup almond milk

1 ½ cups frozen blueberries

Preparation:

Preheat oven 350 C

In a large bowl, mix the melted coconut oil, almond milk, oatmeal powder, ground flax-seeds, desiccated coconut, sugar, baking powder, salt and blueberries.

Spread this mixture to 1 ½ inches high and cut into 15 triangles. Then place them on an oven tray covered with waxed paper. Place in the bottom of the oven and bake for 25 minutes.

Serve with almond chai tea and enjoy!

5

Raw

Macadamia Nut Chocolate Vanilla Fudge

There are literally thousands of chocolate recipes, but this soft and delicious recipe includes macadamia nuts, that when added to cacao butter not only make it a delicious and hearty preparation, but dramatically increase the nutritional value as well.

Preparation for 12 servings

Ingredients:

3 tablespoons coconut water

4 tablespoons of pure water

¾ cup melted coconut butter (not oil)

1 cup peanut butter

1 cup raw macadamias

1 tsp. pure vanilla essence

2 Tbsp. cacao powder

Pinch of sea salt or pink salt

Preparation:

Using a food processor place coconut butter, peanut butter, macadamias, water, vanilla essence, coconut water and salt and process until smooth.

Place half of this mix in a plastic container covered with wax paper or foil and place in fridge for 15 minutes.

Add cacao powder to remaining half of the mixture inside food processor and process until fully mixed.

Remove plastic container from fridge and spread the second mixture over the top of the first layer. Return to fridge and leave for 20 minutes.

Cut into squares and share!

Rainbow Rice Paper Rolls

I always feel that food should not only be healthy, but look good too. It should be, clean, beautiful to the eye, and artistic so that all your senses are enthralled.

First impressions always start with eyes, and so for me, appearance is absolutely critical. And with raw food we have way more options to play with natural colours and freshness of the ingredients. I like to mix vegetables with fruits to create a stunning visual effect. My mother always did the same and it is something I really enjoy.

These rolls are beautiful and tasty.

Preparation for 4 Rolls

Filling Ingredients:

4 sheets of rice paper

½ avocado in sliced

1 Tbsp. dried basil

1 Tbsp. coriander powder

1 mango chopped in small cubes

3 mint leaves

1 tsp. chopped chives

1 peeled and grated carrot

1 cup fresh baby spinach

Sauce Ingredients:

For the sauce (the sauce is essential in this recipe)

1 Tbsp. almond butter or peanut butter

1 Tbsp. lemon juice

1 Tbsp. coconut cream

1 tsp. minced ginger

2 Tbsp. of coconut water

½ tsp of ground cloves

Preparation:

Place the sauce ingredients in a food processor and liquefy until smooth. You want a sauce consistency, if not, add more coconut water.

For the rolls, soak rice paper in a cup of warm water until soft.

When ready, place rice paper on a bench and add the filling ingredients as desired and roll up the wrap like a burrito.

You can then cut them in half using a serrated edge knife to expose the colourful contents. Dip them in the sauce when eating.

Raw Vanilla Cookies

One of the problems faced by vegans and raw vegans is the difficulty in finding decent cookies that meet our dietary preference. This recipe is simple, healthy, delicious and fascinating for children and adults.

Ingredients:

2 Tbsp. coconut oil (melted)

2 Tbsp. almond milk

¼ cup organic sugar or coconut sugar

1 Tbsp. pure vanilla extract

¼ tsp. salt

¾ cup ground oat flour

¾ cup almond flour

¼ cup powdered coconut or cane sugar

¼ cup raisins

Preparation:

Add coconut oil, almond milk, sugar and vanilla into a blender and blend well. Next, transfer this to a food processor and add oat flour, salt and powdered sugar and process until full mixed.

Transfer to a bowl and then mix in all the raisins.

Spread "cookie dough" mix on a tray (½ inch thickness).

Refrigerate and allow to set. Cut into squares.

Optionally, dehydrate for 8 hours at 105 degrees to make a crunchy raw cookie.

Nori Rolls with Creamy Mustard Sauce

If we have guests or a gathering of friends, Nori rolls are a great solution for a tasty and filling "finger food." This recipe is highly nutritious and appetizing even to look at.

With this recipe you will also learn to make a vegan mayonnaise that can accompany many other preparations.

Nori sheets, which is actually made from algae, is famous for its high iodine content.

They are easy to make and pleasing to the eye and palate.

Makes 7 rolls

Ingredients:

Vegan Mayonnaise:

½ cup of coconut water

½ cup walnuts (You can use your favourite nut.
Cashew also works well)

1 tsp. sea salt

2 Tbsp. ground mustard

Filling:

1 cup sunflower seeds soaked in water for 2 hours

1 ½ cups diced celery

¼ red bell pepper, chopped

4 Tbsp. finally chopped cilantro

2 Tbsp. fresh seaweed flakes like dulce

Rolls:

1 nori sheet

2 Tbsp. ground mustard

1 raw diced cucumber

Preparation:

For the mayonnaise: In a food processor mix all ingredients until smooth.

For the filling: Add the ingredients to a food processor and puree until smooth.

To assemble the rolls: Place a sheet of nori on your sushi mat. Sheets of nori have a rough side and a smooth side. Place the nori so that the rough side is facing up.

Place your filling in a line, starting from one inch inside the near side and covering an area of 2 inches. This filling should be no more than ¼ inch thick. Sprinkle 1 tablespoon of mustard powder of the filling, then a thin layer of diced cucumbers and finally a dash of the mayonnaise. Hold the edge of the mat with your thumbs. Start with the edge that has your first ingredient next to it. Lift the nori and fold it over the filling. Make sure to keep the ingredients in place.

Continue to roll the nori sheet. Tuck the front edge of the nori into the roll, and remove the mat as you continue to roll. Roll slowly so that you ensure that the nori roll is coming out even. Add a dash of water to the far edge of the nori sheet to help with sealing the nori roll.

Tighten the roll. You will need to tighten the roll to keep ingredients from falling out when you cut it. Remember to tighten the roll with your sushi mat often, but not too tightly. Roll the nori roll back and forth in the mat to tighten and seal it.

Allow the roll to sit for a minute before cutting it. You can use this time to make your next roll. This waiting period allows the nori to slightly moisten from the filling, which makes it less likely to tear.

Using a very sharp serrated edge knife, cut the nori into five parts.

Place these nori rolls facing up on a plate and garnish as desired.

Triple Goodness Snack

It Adults are just like children, in that we love colours and to eat colourful foods. I think an important part of the food is how much we feel attracted to "eat" with our eyes. This simple recipe is one example.

Makes 6 bars .

Ingredients:

For the base:

1 cup desiccated coconut

¼ cup of soft pitted dates

1 pinch of pink salt or sea salt

2 Tbsp. flax seeds

Strawberry Filling:

2 Tbsp. agave syrup

¾ cup melted coconut butter (not the same as coconut oil)

1 tsp. pure vanilla extract

¼ cup water

½ cup rolled oats

1 cup strawberries

1 Tbsp. lemon juice

1 slice of beet

Vanilla Filling:

2 Tbsp. agave syrup

¾ cup coconut butter (not the same as coconut oil)

1 tsp. pure vanilla extract

½ cup rolled oats

¼ cup water

1 Tbsp. pure vanilla essence

1 pinch of sea salt

Apple Filling:

2 Tbsp. agave syrup

¾ cup coconut butter (not the same as coconut oil)

1 tsp. apple essence

½ cup rolled oats

¼ cup water

1 cup green apple, diced

1 Tbsp. lemon juice

3 leaves of spinach

Preparation:

To make the base mix all base ingredients in a food processor until the mixture pulls away from the side.

In a 4x4 cm tray covered in coconut oil, spread the mixture to form a base of about ½ inch thick or a little less and place in the refrigerator.

Next mix the apple filling thoroughly in a food processor.

Next, take the base from the fridge and add the apple mixture and take it back to the refrigerator for 10 minutes. Then mix the vanilla filling in a food processor and add on top of the apple filling.

Repeat for the strawberry filling.

When ready, remove from the refrigerator and the cut into bars or squares.

6

Desserts

Chia Summer Pudding

This is a very popular dessert in my courses on vegan cuisine and one of the favourite desserts of my students. I love the freshness of acidic fruits. This is a simple dessert to make and also raw and vegan.

Recipe for 4 people

Ingredients:

2 cups of chia seeds

2 cups almond milk

2 Tbsp. sweetener (preferably coconut sugar

or agave syrup)

1 cup of coconut cream

1 passion fruit

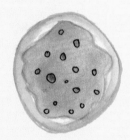

Preparation:

Combine the almond milk and chia seeds in a bowl and place it in the refrigerator. Leave in the fridge for 4 hours, but every 20 or 30 minutes or so gently stir.

When the chia seeds and almond milk have a gelatinous consistency, stir in the coconut cream and sweetener.

Return the mix to the fridge for another 30 minutes.

Serve garnished with a little more passion fruit.

Classic and Healthy Vegan Truffles

TRUFFLES! Who wants truffles? Nothing beats the delicious feeling of soft chocolate in our mouth! Truffles can take on various forms, but let's try 3 simple but elegant combinations. All are healthy and tasty!

Recipe for 4 people.

Ingredients:

¼ cup coconut cream

2 Tbsp. grated raw cacao butter

¼ cup cacao powder

¼ cup agave syrup or maple syrup

And for the variations:

1 tsp. chopped walnuts

1 tsp. desiccated coconut

1 tsp. ground cinnamon

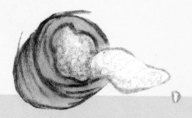

Preparation:

Melt the cacao butter in a pot that is sitting inside another pan full of hot water. Once melted, pour into a food processor, add cacao powder, coconut cream and syrup and blend everything until thoroughly mixed.

Using a spoon scoop portions into your hand and roll into balls.

Optionally, you can add cinnamon powder, desiccated coconut, or nuts. I also like to cover the truffles with cherries.

These truffles can be refrigerated for up to two weeks.

These are a great party snack for children, with the added benefit of being nutritionally powerful.

Vegan Raspberry Jelly

It is not easy to find the right mix for a soft, juicy and perfect vegan jelly. The main component of jelly is gelatine, which is derived from animal bones and fats. If we want our children to enjoy healthy dessert, free from animal abuse, then this nutritious and cruelty-free jelly is the answer.

Recipe for 4 people.

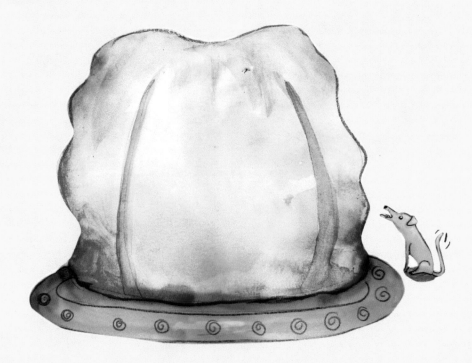

Ingredients:

1 tsp. cornstarch

2 Tbsp. water

4 cups raspberry juice (or your favourite
sweet fruit blended)

1 tsp. agar-agar

Preparation:

In a bowl, dissolve cornstarch in water and let it sit for a few minutes.

In a saucepan, mix one-half cup of blueberry juice and agar-agar, let stand for 5 minutes and then cook over medium-low heat for 1 minute.

Next, using a whisk mix in the cornstarch and remaining juice to the hot blueberry juice.

Transfer to another container and place in the fridge for 4 hours to set. Enjoy!

Chocolate Oat Snack Bars

I like nutritious food that I can take
with me everywhere.
 On a plant-based diet, sometimes
when we are away from home, it is not
easy to find healthy snack foods, so I
try to bring my own yummy snacks.
These bars are perfect to take with you
anywhere.

Makes 2 dozen bars

Ingredients:

1 cup sifted flour (barley, oat, or wheat)

1 cup coconut sugar or brown sugar

1 tsp. salt

½ tsp. baking powder

1 cup oats

½ cup raisins

1 Tbsp. vanilla extract

¾ cup sunflower oil

½ cup non-dairy milk

1 cup cacao powder

Preparation:

Pre heat the oven to 350 C.

Mix the flour, salt, cacao powder and baking powder in a bowl.

Then add the sugar, rolled oats, raisins, vanilla extract and non-dairy milk.

Mix everything well and then spread onto a baking tray about 2 inches high.

Bake in oven for 15 minutes, or until it is golden brown. Let cool and cut into bars.

Lemon Vanilla Energy Bar

I'm a big fan of acid fruits. They have a certain tartness that makes you feel more energetic and fresh. In aromatherapy, essences that are the acidic, such as orange and lemon, give the body more energy. Alchemically, acidic fruits increase fire in the body, making them much easier to digest.

Makes 10 lemon bars

Ingredients:

4 tablespoons melted vegan butter or
melted coconut oil

2 cups brown sugar or coconut sugar

2 tsp. lemon zest

½ cup fresh lemon juice

2 Tbsp. agave syrup

1 tsp. vanilla (pure essence)

1 tsp. sea salt

4 soft dates

2 Tbsp. sifted wheat flour

2 cup sifted wheat flour

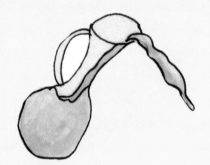

Preparation:

The bars have two layers. To make the bottom crispy, crunchy layer:

Preheat oven to 300 ° C

In the food processor, mix the vegan butter, dates, brown sugar, lemon zest, 2 cups of wheat flour and salt. In an oven tray, covered with waxed paper, spread this mixture until it is even and let it bake for 20-25 minutes until golden brown.

In a bowl, mix the sugar, lemon juice, agave syrup, vanilla essence, 2 Tbsp. flour and salt. This mixture is placed on top of the bottom later when ready. Bake again for 20 minutes.

Take out of the oven and allow to cool. Carefully remove wax paper and cut into bars.

Smoothie

Berry Powerful Smoothie

I love smoothies! You can make them look and taste like melted ice cream with heavenly flavours. But when made the right way, they are also nutritious and energising.

Let's start with this berry powerful smoothie, which has a mix of red and green fruits so it is also visually stimulating.

Banana is one of the most important base ingredients of a good smoothie, to this we add sweet berries to make our smoothie high in antioxidants, anti-inflammatory, low in calories, and so perfect to start the day. This dramatic smoothie comes in two parts.

Ingredients:

Part 1 (red base)

¼ fresh beet, grated

½ cup strawberries

½ cup blackberries

½ cup coconut milk

1 fresh dates

More non-dairy milk or water as needed

Part 2 (green top)

1 cup fresh coconut water

2 kiwi fruits

1 cup chopped spinach

¼ cup almond milk

1 banana

1 fresh dates

More non-dairy milk or water as needed

Preparation:

Mix Part 1 adding the necessary water or non-dairy milk as needed to make a creamy consistency. Pour in glasses until half full.

Then do the same with the Part 2, then pour this mixture into the same glasses until they are filled to the top. The result should be a red base and a green top.

Garnish with kiwi slices, or strawberries and blackberries.

Mango, Kale Super Smoothie

Who does not like mango? With a variety of shapes, flavours and textures to be found around the world, this exotic fruit has become a universal favourite.

But kale, why? That sounds boring. Well, maybe if you ate it alone, but when blended into this smoothie the mango takes command of the flavour, but you'll still get the powerful nutritional benefits of the kale. Kale is rich in fiber, low in calories, high in potassium and iron, loaded with antioxidants, as well as vitamin A and vitamin C, and has more calcium by weight than cow's milk. Wow, what a superfood!

Ingredients:

½ cup coconut milk

¼ tsp. vanilla extract

2 Tbsp. fresh coconut meat

1 cup chopped kale

10 peppermint or mint leaves

1 cup frozen mango

2 Tbsp. almond flour

Water or non-dairy milk as needed

Preparation:

Blend until creamy and enjoy without fear!

Morning Zinger Smoothie

Smoothies can be a divine mix of playful colours to make them as appealing to the eye as they are healthy for our body.

Fresh cherries are considered a "super food" because they are full of antioxidants help reduce the chances of heart disease or cancer. And last but not least, they are among the few fruits that contains melatonin. Oranges are a great source of vitamin C and antioxidants.

Ingredients:

Bottom layer

½ cup soy or coconut yogurt

½ banana

½ cup fresh orange juice

Top layer

½ cup soy or coconut yogurt

½ banana

½ cup almond milk

1 cup fresh cherries

Preparation:

Separately blend each layer until smooth. Half fill each glass with the orange bottom layer and then the top cherry layer. Garnish with a cherry and/or a slice of orange.

Macadamia Ice Cream Smoothie

I know what you're thinking…what is this amazing smoothie? This perfect combination of ice cream and a smoothie! Delicious, divine, healthy and charming.

Macadamia nuts are rich in potassium, phosphorus and magnesium, and a high energy source, in addition to being loaded with antioxidants. This is a great smoothie to start your day.

Ingredients:

5 Frozen Bananas

3 tablespoons peanut butter

1 cup macadamias (soaked overnight)

½ cup almond milk

¼ cup of pure water

Preparation:

Blend until smooth. Place in a glass and if desired you can also garnish with cacao nibs as chocolate chips and one mint leaf.

Caramel Apple Smoothie

Who does not remember those moments in youth enjoying a caramel apple!

Ignoring large amounts of unhealthy sugar, I have an improvement on the traditional recipe, so you can be sure it is healthy for your children, delicious and even yummy for adults.

Pink lady apples are highly digestible, tasty and refreshing…and adding caramel sauce to them is like a dream.

Ingredients:

Smoothie

½ cup apple juice

1 frozen banana

4 ice cubes

Caramelized Apple Sauce

1 Pink Lady apple, peeled, cored and sliced

into half circles

½ cup organic sugar

2 Tbsp. water

Preparation:

Blend apple juice, banana and ice cubes until smooth. Pour smoothie into glasses.

In a plan, cook sugar and water on a low flame until the sugar caramelizes.

Dip the apple slices into this caramel sauce and garnish the smoothie.

Recipes for Animals

Doggy Peanut butter, Pumpkin Cookies

For our furry four-legged friends, these cookies are a welcome delight. They are good for their health too. And don't they deserve a treat once in a while, even though they eat our shoes?

Win a lick from your best friend with this cookie recipe.

Recipe for 30 cookies

Ingredients:

3 tsp. grated raw pumpkin

2 tsp. baking powder

1 cup grated raw carrots

2 tsp. dried dates, sliced

½ cup natural peanut butter

1 ½ wheat flour

½ cup rolled oats

½ cup filtered water

Preparation:

Preheat oven to 325 ° C

In a bowl, mix flour, oats and baking powder. Make a hole in the middle.

In another bowl, add the carrots, pumpkin, dates, peanut butter and water.

Combine contents of both bowls and mix well.

Spread the cookie dough and use your favourite cookie cutter to make the cookie shapes.

Place cookies on an over tray dusted with flour and bake for 14-16 minutes.

Allow to cool and serve to your best friend.

Biography of Juliana Castaneda

Juliana Castaneda was born in Colombia. At age 5, Juliana adopted a vegetarian diet and at age 9 was already cooking meals for the family under the guidance of her mother. She visited and lived in many Bhakti yoga temples in South and Central America as a young girl, and was fascinated by the idea of cooking with devotion and purifying her meals with mantras.

At age 23, Juliana return to Colombia and with the help of her long time friend Ekala Isvara, she founded the first and only vegan animal sanctuary in the Andes Mountains called *Para-matma*, in which 34 animals are cared for, including a cow and an ox, making it the only animal shelter in Colombia that protects cows.

Along with giving public talks in South America on animal protection, Juliana continues to develop her culinary skills as she visits different countries and is currently a student Australian born, Paul Rodney Turner, the "Food Yogi."

Juliana has held regular gourmet vegan cooking courses in Colombia for the last 6 years and through her teaching, she also tries to instill in her students the importance of food in one's spiritual development.

Juliana is now a certified animal reiki and aromatherapy healer and has been a student and practitioner of bhakti yoga for more than 26 years. She is currently the coordinator for FFL in South America and assistant to the director of Food For Life Global, the world's largest vegan food relief.

At age 24, she was initiated into Bhakti yoga, a spiritual path of devotion to God, and received the name Jagannatha Priya dasi, which means she was the "servant of and dear to "the Lord of the Universe."

Today, Juliana and Ekala still manage the **Paramatma Animal Sanctuary.**

Along with giving public talks in South America on animal protection, Juliana continues to develop her culinary skills as she visits different countries and is currently a student Australian born, Paul Rodney Turner, the "Food Yogi."

Juliana has held regular gourmet vegan cooking courses in Colombia for the last 6 years and through her teaching, she also tries to instill in her students the importance of food in one's spiritual development.

Juliana is now a certified animal reiki and aromatherapy healer and has been a student and practitioner of bhakti yoga for more than 26 years. She is currently the coordinator for Food for Life in South America and assistant to the director of Food For Life Global.

Biography of Jennyfer Rodriguez A.

Jennyfer was born in Bogota, Colombia and majored in graphic design. She later realized that her passion was
illustration, so she decided to focus exclusively on deveoping her unique illustration style.

She is a long-time vegetarian, animal lover (especially dogs) and lives with two of her "best friends,"
Suka and Kira. She loves to watch movies, read, draw and create new characters from other worlds.

She has participated in exhibitions such as "Mujer, Memorias, salón de ilsutración Libertadores of 2013"
and has been published in Fanzines as "Etcetera street edition."

You can find her work at:

www.jennrodriguez1321.wix.com/jennrodriguez

www.jennrodriguezilustradora.blogspot.com/

www.facebook.com/jennilustraciones

For more information:

If you need more information about this book or my work.

contact@cocinandoconjaggy.com

Blog

www.cocinandoconjaggy.com

Facebook

www.facebook.com/veganjags

Paramatma Animal Sanctuary

ParamatmaFarm.com

Situated in the Andes Mountains, this vegan shelter is home to 34 animals

Printed in Great Britain
by Amazon.co.uk, Ltd.,
Marston Gate.